Coming soon from Paul Figueroa

Book two in the Your Life is Calling series:

The Journey to Purpose

Book three in the Your Life is Calling series:

The Journey to Meaning

Personal workbooks for the Your Life is Calling series:

The Journey Home
The Journey to Meaning
The Journey to Purpose

Paul is also available for speaking engagements on these and a myriad of other topics.

See www.PaulFigueroa.com for more information.

Listen

Your Life is Calling

The Journey Home

Book One of the
YOUR LIFE IS CALLING SERIES

by Paul Figueroa

1

Brian was a young man of twenty-eight when the dreams started. By everyone else's standards he was tremendously happy. He was married to his high school sweetheart and former cheerleader, Melinda. They lived in a wonderful two story home at the end of a quiet cul-de-sac in Redmond, Washington, not far from Seattle and he had a budding career with a booming tech startup he helped create. From the outside, it looked like a dream life.

On the inside, the dreams were wreaking havoc on him. They had started in the fall and had been haunting him ever since. At first, Brian thought they were just the typical "doom and gloom" dreams that show up because of the dreary Seattle weather. After the third week, he started to take notice. You see, it had been the same three dreams - over and over and over again.

The first was him in a drowning ship. He could almost make out the sinking ship's name, yet it just eluded him each night. It would start off with him getting aboard as a young boy, eight years old to be exact. He was with his mom and his stepdad and they were taking a tour of Hawaii. Everything started off great, on the surface. They were happy and jovial as they met the other two couples taking the tour. Brian's mom, Jennifer, introduced him with the "Proud Mom" smile and his stepdad, Jerry, was mingling with the other dads. He was certain they were talking business, Jerry always did.

They set out from the marina and he was happy as could be, then a feeling of foreboding would come over the young Brian. It was right before a sudden storm jerked, smashed and spun him, his mom, dad and everyone else on the ship around like a cork. The salty smell and chill of green sea water filled his senses. He would wake up each time sweating right as he was taken below and knocked unconscious in the galley. He would wake up feeling like he was punched in the gut, like he had water in his lungs and was unable to breathe.

His second dream wasn't much better. He was in his home on Maui, where he was spending his retirement. He was around sixty-five in this dream, healthy and full of life for a man of any age. It was a Tuesday afternoon in this one. He left for his usual walk at 2:30 p.m. You see, that's when the deli on the corner made its freshest pot of Kona Blend coffee, his favorite. He would leave wearing his khaki shorts and his favorite yellow and beige Hawaiian shirt - everything was wonderful. It was sunny, perfectly warm and he had a spring in his step as he pecked Melinda on the cheek on his way out the door. The problem didn't start until he got home, or at least, until he tried to go home.

After he had his coffee, he went back to his complex, the Spring Estates. He walked up to his door, unit 34, and the door would be locked and his key wouldn't work.

Panic sinks in as a young Latin woman opens the door, sleepy, and asks, "May I help you?"

"What are you doing in my home? Where is my wife?" Brian asks.

"I'm sorry sir, I don't know what you're talking about. Why are you banging on my door?"

The knot in Brian's stomach grows and he starts to feel a wave of nausea. He looks past the woman and sees similar furniture to what he remembers, yet, he feels something is very wrong. He starts to get queasy and then abruptly wakes up, panting and looking around to get his bearings.

You might notice how only one of these recurring dreams would be enough for anybody. In Brian's case, there's one more.

His final dream starts off in sunny Florida. He's heading off on a cruise ship to the Caribbean with his wife and a son he's never met in real life, Brian Jr. The boy in this dream is about seven and he's the spitting image of Brian. Same eyes. Same smile. Cute as a bug.

They're running late and their town car scurries to the drop off area, letting them off with plenty of time... but there's never enough time for Brian. He shuffles his wife and son to the staging area for the cruise. There he's met by, you guessed it, lines of people being herded to seven ticket takers via stanchions with retractable cloth belts. Moo.

Once he gets to the counter, he gets irate at the luggage clerk. You see, he's spent the past thirty minutes thinking of all the things that were wrong with the operation. Not enough clerks, very little space and if they would just let people pre-pay for a precheck process, he wouldn't have to waste any of his precious time.

During his thirty minute mental tirade he missed the fact that his son was having a wonderful time. Junior was talking with people nearby, asking questions and making friends. He was aglow with the newness and intrigue of this wonderful experience. He was "tickled pink."

Brian lights into the poor clerk, who starts to tear up. He doesn't notice her at all and asks to speak to a supervisor. Melinda is begging him to calm down. All she gets is, "I'll take care of this."

This exchange leads to the usual outcome, some embarrassment for Melinda, Brian Jr. soaking it all in, and a comped meal for big Brian's troubles.

His dream progresses to him being in full tuxedo at the dinner table with the Captain. There, he has a "few drinks" with dinner and starts complaining about the service and the food. The Captain is sitting next to him, and amidst a disingenuous smile, he tells Brian that he'll look into it.

Brian can't stop his brain or the complaining. All he can think about is problems at work, not having enough money, regrets he has from decisions he's made and he's noticing everything wrong on the ship. Everything. Every thing. He has another drink, to "calm his nerves and wind down."

The next thing he knows, he's watching himself have a full blown verbal argument with his wife. The Captain is watching along with everyone else at the dining table, including his son, Brian Jr. Brian sees himself irate, belligerent and angry at everything. His "in body" self leaves in a huff with a full drink in his hand.

His viewpoint changes and he's able to watch what happens next. Melinda apologizes profusely to the cruise captain and kneels down to Jr's level, kissing him on the cheek and telling him, "It'll be okay. Daddy's under quite a bit of stress. He loves you."

A quick burst of blue light covers everything in the room and Brian notices Melinda is talking, but her lips aren't moving. "God I love that man. I don't know what happened to him. I'm so glad I can talk with...   At least I know he loves me. God, I feel guilty."

Brian's stomach flips. She's having an affair. Sweat starts forming on his brow along with a feeling of anger, guilt and remorse.

"Why is he so mean to me?" It's little Brian's thoughts now. "Why is he so mean to everyone? Maybe if I do better. I can be a better boy, a good boy. That will fix things. I'm so scared when he gets mad. I'll make sure to get all my chores done - even before they're due, and I'll do a better job in school. That'll make daddy happy. I'll be a good little boy."

He wakes up at this point each time. He has a familiar knot in his stomach and this foreboding feeling that there is something too, too, familiar about this.

The more he thinks about these dreams, the worse he feels. He started getting headaches and frankly, doesn't know what to do.

He didn't dare tell Melinda, he didn't want to ruin what they had and she was very logical in her thinking. She wouldn't be able to help him with this.

He knew it was a matter of time before she stopped taking, "I'm fine, it's just insomnia" for an answer and he was having a hard time concentrating at work, too.

Tick, tock. Tick. Tock.

2

It was a dreary Wednesday evening when Brian pulled into his usual parking spot at Mobile Tech Web Solutions. It was 8:10 p.m. and he was late for the meeting. He rushed upstairs, said a hasty "Hello" to Ben, the night guard, and scurried to the elevator. He activated the 12th floor with his key card and was whisked to it. As the door opens, the hallways are eerily quiet. He runs to the main conference room. He's in luck, they haven't started the video conference yet. He took his seat next to his partner and good friend, Chuck Hamilton, and made his apologies.

"No problem, Brian. You made it just in time," remarked Chuck. "You have the figures for the upcoming merger, yes?"

Brian's heart sank for a minute, then he remembered he had them on a thumb drive on his key ring. He had been forgetting things quite a bit lately, so he'd gotten into the habit of backing things up much more than normal.

"You bet!" he said. Brian fumbled in his pockets and found his thumb drive, secretly praying it was on there. As he was booting up his laptop, the monitor in the room switched from its Samsung screen saver to that of a board room in Singapore.

They get to come in at a normal time, he thought.

As Windows launched, he opened the file explorer and found the file he was looking for. He let out a sigh of relief.

Underneath all the hub bub, this was an exciting time. They were finalizing the discussions of a multimillion-dollar merger and Brian was to be a very rich man. He started the PowerPoint, connected it to the video conference and his stomach flipped. He was looking at the board room in Singapore, past the five men that were dressed in oddly similar blue suits. Behind the man at the head of the table, Mr. Ang, was a model of a ship. The same type of ship that he drowned in during his first dream.

Sweat started to form on his forehead and the knot in his stomach showed up again. "What is going on?" he blurted out loud.

Chuck looked at him quizzically. "You got what you need?" Chuck asked.

"Yeah," Brian said. "Sorry."

The meeting progressed with Chuck covering the profit and loss statements for the last seven years as Brian mindlessly flipped through the PowerPoint at the prearranged time. Mr. Ang asked for the five, seven and ten-year projection figures and Brian clicked until they showed up.

Inside Brian's head, he was spinning and fogging up a bit.

How could this be? he asked himself.

Maybe it's not the same ship. It could be a coincidence, he thought.

As things were wrapping down, Chuck was noticeably happy and optimistic. "Mr. Ang," Brian said, "I couldn't help noticing the ship you have on display behind you. My father was a Merchant Marine for twenty years and I couldn't, well...what kind is it?" he asked.

"Thank you for asking, Mr. Richardson, it's a Lagoon Catamaran. Her name is Deep Insight. She's a forty-footer and I'm very fond of her."

The knot in the pit of Brian's stomach felt like it weighed 400 pounds. He noticed his forehead was wet from the sweat that had formed there. A sudden wave of nausea came over him.

"She's beautiful, Mr. Ang."

"Thank you."

The business concluded and Brian's brain was flat. It was as if he was on a remote desert island with no stimulus. Just emptiness.

"Brian. Brian!" Chuck said. Brian's brain seemed to reboot and he was aware that the conference was over. Chuck was standing up, looking at him with a puzzled and worried expression on his face.

"You okay, man? What happened? It's like you checked out after that stupid boat question. What was that about, by the way? Your father was never in the Merchant Marines."

"I'm not sure," Brian replied. "It looked oddly familiar and I wanted to find out about it. You ever had one of those feelings you've seen something before?"

"What is the matter with you?" Chuck asked. "You've been acting weird for the last couple of months, I'm not liking it. We have a chance to be rich men here, Brian. Don't mess it up."

"Sorry," Brian said. He was apologizing way more often of late and frankly, not liking it.

That night, Brian got home around midnight. The house was cold and dark. He slipped off his shoes, poured himself a half full glass of bourbon, took a pull and sat down in his favorite chair in the living room.

Am I losing it? he wondered.

He took another gulp of his drink. It started to numb him a bit. A familiar and often sought after feeling of his for the last few months.

Dang, what's going on? What is going on? He finished the rest of his glass and fell asleep.

He woke up at 6:00 a.m. to the rustling of Melinda in the kitchen. She was making her morning coffee. A feeling of shame came over him as he stood up. He felt the desire to go into the kitchen, walk up behind her and hug her for several minutes.

He headed up to their room to shower instead.

As he stepped in, he felt the intense warmth of the shower hit his body and a wave of relief came over him. All of a sudden, the dream on the ship started – only this time he was awake for it. He smelled the marine air as he was walking up to the boat as a young boy. He was holding his mom's hand and he noticed how the boards of the dock were so clean and tidy. He heard his dad talking with a man behind him. He was sharing his dream of retiring someday, of "Hitting it so big, they'll have to buy me out!" His dad was laughing.

As they reached the back of the boat, he asked his mom what the name of the boat was.

I'm not sure," she said. "Let's look." His mom's hand guided them to the back of the boat as he looked to see the words "Deep Insight" in black cursive.

Brian snapped out of the dream right as his knees buckled and he hit the bottom of the bath tub, hard. He started to cry uncontrollably as a wave of fear moved through his body.

"What the hell is happening? What the HELL is happening!?" he yelled.

Seconds passed into minutes, and he looked up to see a concerned Melinda looking down at him. "Brian, are you okay?"

"I'm good Melinda, I'm good. It's been a long week. I must have slipped."

"You look awful," she remarked. "Why don't you come down and have breakfast with me? I'm off to Brazil tomorrow and I'd like to spend some time with you before I go."

"Sure. Sure. Give me a few minutes. I'll be right down." As she walked away, Brian thought how hot she looked in her business attire.

Man, he thought, *I'm one lucky guy. How did I ever hook her?*

One of the problems with this kind of thinking is that it drives the idea of sharing what's going on deep, deep, deep down. He thought that if she had any idea of what was happening, she'd be gone. That's one of the negative effects of forgetting who we are and choosing to not be vulnerable. Hopefully, he'll learn this lesson, before it's too late.

3

They spent some time together at breakfast. There was a problem, though. Brian was adrift in fear and not present at all. He was preoccupied with his recurring dreams, his fear, thoughts of the merger and of losing Melinda.

Was she having an affair? he thought. The knot in his stomach was back.

As Melinda was talking to him about her upcoming trip, his thoughts were consumed with:

How did I luck out?

What did she see in me?

He topped it off with, *If I tell her what's going on, she's outa here!*

As she continued to talk, he noticed how her eyes sparkled when she spoke of dancing, Brazil and the moonlight walks they once had there. He felt his heart open up and the desire to reach out and kiss her swelled within him.

Stop it! he thought. *Stop it!*

He immediately started to think of her with another man and all those feelings quickly left him. He turned to stone, acted as if he was listening and then planned his day in his mind while she kept talking.

He came out of it as she said, "Okay, bye honey. Have a great day," and she kissed him on his cheek. Dazed, confused, scared and angry was his current state of being.

I need a drink, he thought as he heard the front door close.

He poured himself another bourbon, took out a legal pad and began to write.

> *Why are my dreams coming?*
>
> *What do they mean?*

Psychiatrist? Am I going crazy? Is she having an affair?

I got this, he thought.

The following words came out of his pen.

> Step 1: Complete the merger. This will be done within one
>
> week.
>
> Step 2: Find a psychiatrist, a good one!
>
> Step 3: I have no idea.

He backed the rest of his bourbon, feeling a bit queasy this time, and went up and took a shower.

As he got dressed for work, he couldn't stop thinking about that boat.

Deep Insight, what kind of name is that? Deep Insight...

He remembered he had a ten o'clock with Chuck to review the figures and the timeline for their business. He figured he had enough time to swing by QFC and get some more bourbon on the way. He went down to the kitchen and found an old silver flask that his dad had. He filled it with the remaining bourbon, tossed the bottle, grabbed his briefcase and headed to the store.

As he was in line waiting to purchase his "Keep it together" liquid, he glanced up at the tabloids. There, in bright bold yellow letters were the words: "Man dies in sinking ship. Four others feared dead."

Those things are so fake, he thought.

He bought his bourbon and took a hit in his car before he tossed it in the back seat and scurried off to work.

"Ah," he said. "I got this!"

He sat down in Chuck's office, who laid out some bad news.

"We've got a major problem. Our fiscal figures for the third and fourth quarter last year are off, I mean way off. This will cost us our merger."

"How did that happen?" Brian asked.

"Our bookkeeper, Barb, made several mistakes. She covered it up pretty well until I noticed it last night. Honestly, when she handed me the Profit and Loss sheets, I had a feeling something was off. I couldn't put a finger on it until last night."

"Can we fix it?"

"Yes, but not legally. If anyone finds out, we'll be in prison."

"What, exactly, are we talking about?

"We'll have to fake some invoices, fudge the accounts receivable and pray to God they don't back trace it to our customers. As long as they don't look too deep, no one will be the wiser. All of our projections were based on those figures."

"Okay, what do you need from me?" Brian asked.

They talked for over an hour and Brian walked out with a plan. He ignored that nagging ache in his stomach, took a pull from his dad's flask and stuck to the plan. The plan. The plan. The plan.

For the next two days, Brian lived the plan. He created the invoices, faked signatures and doctored the books.

I got this!

His confidence grew along with his bourbon consumption. There was a direct relationship as a matter of fact. He began to pour it in his coffee and hide bottles at home.

I'll only do this until the merger goes through, he thought.

It was 8:45 in the evening when Melinda pulled up. He heard the garage door open and close. The click of her heels always brought a smile to his face.

"Hi Babe," she said.

"Hey. How was your day?"

"Good. Anything on TV?"

"Not really. Same ol' same ol'."

"K. I'm gonna shower and get to bed. I have to get up early tomorrow to pack for my flight."

"Sounds good." Brian took another pull from his crystal glass of bourbon.

He noticed a quiet, soft, distant voice come from inside him. "Talk to her," it whispered.

God, I'm losing my mind, he thought as he backed his glass.

He was awakened at 4:45 a.m. by the sound of Melinda quietly opening her suitcase in the walk-in closet. She was humming softly to herself.

God, I love her. Then, he realized his head was throbbing. *Too much bourbon,* he thought.

He decided to get up and spend a few minutes with her before she left.

They had a wonderful light breakfast together. He helped her load her bags into the trunk of her 450 SL, gave her a long kiss and as she got into the car, he had a weird feeling. She shut the door and the sound was almost deafening. He stood in the garage, dazed, as she backed her car out onto the street and drove away.

Bourbon. Bourbon. He poured himself a glass, backed it, poured another and showered, shampooed and shaved.

He came to at his desk in Redmond. Fast at it again, they had a deadline for a receivable with a customer in Taiwan. The coding was off and his software testing people couldn't tell him why. It occurred to him that if this became a glitch, it would be one more reason for the merger to fail.

After four hours of ardent keystrokes, coding and decoding, Brian took a break. For some reason he felt like heading down to the corner deli for lunch. He hadn't been there in years. He quickly dismissed it. He went to the bathroom instead, checked to make sure it was empty and took a pull off his dad's flask. He splashed some water on his face, looked at himself and whispered, "I got this," and went back to work.

He began clicking away on his laptop when Chuck showed up in his doorway. "We've got another problem. Barbara just quit."

"Jesus," Brian said. "What next? I can't help you, Chuck. I'm knee deep in this coding and frankly, it's got me beat right now."

"Great, just great." Chuck quickly turned, stormed out and slammed the door behind him.

Bourbon. What else could go wrong?

Right as that thought left him, his cell phone rang. It was his mom. She hardly ever calls. "Hi Mom, what's up?"

"It's Jerry. He's in the hospital. He's had a stroke."

Silence. Stone. Cold. Silence.

"Brian, are you there?"

"Yes mom, I'm here. How bad is it?" His mind flooded with thoughts of all the things that were going on. He quickly flashed to the sinking boat, Mr. Ang, Melinda, a courtroom where the falsified invoicing and deliverables were on display, his stepdad in a hospital bed, Melinda getting married to another man and a grave with his own name on it.

He swiped right on his phone, ending the call with his mom.

What the… What the?

He took a pull off the flask. He was now officially, from the inside out, numb.

4

He awoke the next morning at 2:30 a.m. It was abrupt and it felt like someone was in the room with him. He felt his heart pound and flicked on the light on his bed stand.

"Who's there? WHO IS THERE?" he shouted.

Silence.

No one could have gotten in you idiot. The alarm didn't go off.

Stupid!

One more pull off the flask.

I might as well get up and see if I can finish that coding.

He threw on a t-shirt and slippers and headed down to his den. He couldn't shake the feeling of someone being there with him.

Knock it off, he thought. *No one is in here.*

He fired up his Toshiba and started to work. In the background of his home page, a video started playing. "400 passengers of flight BA716 are feared dead. Authorities say they lost contact with the aircraft at 11:14 a.m. local time somewhere over the Atlantic Ocean. All are feared lost. As we…"

A wave of fear engulfed Brian.

What flight was she on? What flight was she on? Oh my God!

He ran over to her desk and frantically looked through it, looking for anything to tell him what flight she was on.

BA716. BA716. Crap, nothing

He went back to his desk. He looked up her airline and flight departure time out of SeaTac.

Flight BA716. Flight BA716.

He clicked frantically with his mouse. One final click.

Flight BA716 from Atlanta. Damnit. That doesn't help.

The knot welled up in his stomach again. He remembered her saying she had a connecting flight from Atlanta. He went to her email account and found the confirmation email.

Flight CL417 leaves SeaTac at 7:36 a.m. Flight BA716 from Atlanta…

Oh my God!

Brian sank in his chair and started sobbing.

He was awakened an hour later by a loud rapping at his door. The rap became a bang.

"Brian! Brian!"

It was Chuck. He let the banging continue for several minutes. The banging stopped and he heard footsteps outside his window. The banging continued on the window by his desk.

"Brian, damn it! I know you're in there!"

Go away, he thought. *Go away.*

After several minutes, the banging stopped and he heard the sound of Chuck leaving in his red Jaguar.

Brian felt immobilized. Like a deer in headlights, he was stunned and unable to move. So much has happened in the last few days, his brain flat out could not handle it. It was as if it shut off for his own safety. Nothing in his brain. Nothing.

He became aware of his breathing. It was slow and rhythmic. In, out. In, out. As he focused on his breathing, things started to become clear. Things were occurring to him, they weren't thoughts really, they were more like "insights" or "knowings." It was as if his brain was now listening to a different cable channel.

For some reason, he felt the strong urge to go the café by his work. It was more than an urge, something was compelling him.

Ok. Ok. I'll go.

He put his silver flask in the inside coat pocket of his leather coat and got into his blue Range Rover. He backed out slowly, noticing his brain was still mostly quiet, and started to the café.

He arrived 45 minutes later and realized his desire for bourbon had dwindled. He patted his coat pocket looking for the rigid reassurance of its presence, and went inside. He suddenly became hungry for a BLT. He hadn't had one of those in years. He approached the clerk, ordered and paid. He glanced around and found a nice table at the far end of the café, in the corner by the window. He got some water and sat down.

He reflected for a few minutes, trying to decipher if he was numb or at peace. He really couldn't tell. The waitress came by, set down his sandwich and asked if there was anything else he wanted.

"No thanks," he said.

"Okay honey," she replied. She gave him a quick wink and walked off.

No one's called me honey in years.

Right as he bit into his sandwich, the bell above the café door rang as it opened. He noticed an older man entering the café wearing a fedora and beige and brown tweed sport coat. A feeling of comfort came over him.

He continued to eat as he watched the older man order. He seemed to be way too happy for anyone's own good. He smiled and joked with the clerk. They both laughed and he went over to the soda fountain and poured himself an orange soda. He seemed to glow with joy.

Weird.

The old man walked right to him and asked, "This seat taken, Son?"

"No. No. No one's sitting here," Brian heard himself say.

"Thanks." He sat down next to him and started to whistle an oddly familiar song.

Brian started to cry. Again.

Why am I crying? he thought. *What is going on?*

The tears seemed to open up a part of Brian, with a slow steady creak, much like an old door that's been closed for years and years. It started slowly, then opened up into a fluid stream of reassurance, peace and warmth.

"Hi Brian, my name is Phillip. Glad to meet you."

"What was that song you were whistling?"

"Oh, some tune from many years ago. Like it?"

"I'm not sure," he hesitated. "Who are you?"

"I'm just a man, no different than you. The question is... who are you?"

"What do you mean, who am I? What kind of person asks a stranger that? Excuse me, I need to leave."

"You can, Brian, but things will get worse until you listen."

"What do you mean listen? Who are you? How do you know my name? Get out of my way old man."

As he said the words, he knew he didn't mean them. There was something about this old guy. Something reassuring and comforting.

None of this made sense though. None of it.

"Get out of my way!" Brian stormed out of the café and got into his car. He reached for his flask, took a long pull and headed to work.

He pulled into his assigned parking spot and noticed there were several Redmond PD squad cars parked out front and a couple of obviously unmarked police vehicles.

Now what?

This time it was a bit different. His knees started shaking and he was afraid. From the core of his being, afraid. Another pull on the flask.

He ran to the elevator and headed to the 12th floor. As the doors of the elevator started to open he resisted the urge to try and force them shut. He was expecting the worst, a floor full of police.

The doors finally opened and everything looked normal. He kept it together until he got to his office. He shut the door, sat down, put his head in his hands and started crying - from the depths of his being - he cried.

He took a deep breath, pulled on the flask and pulled out his cell phone. He called the airlines and asked to talk with the Public Information Officer. He was given the run around until he screamed into his Samsung, "MY WIFE WAS ON THAT PLANE DAMN IT!" He was told he would be connected and put on hold.

A sweet young voice turned off the automated phone music.

"This is Charlie Simpson, Public Information Officer. May I help you?"

Brian immediately noticed the southern accent. He explained that he thought his wife was on the plane.

"I'm sorry Mr. Richardson, we're unable to release any information unless it's through channels initiated on our end. I hope you understand."

"My wife was on that plane," he said through his clenched teeth.

"I'm sorry sir. As we have said through the media, as it stands now we've been unable to locate our aircraft and all the passengers are presumed missing. Rescue teams are in the area trying to ascertain the status of the aircraft. Policy dictates we wait 72 hours before we make an official announcement as to their status.   I'm sorry."

Brian hung up, almost throwing the phone through the wall.

5

Knock. Knock. Knock.

It was Chuck at his door. He walked in, smiling.

"I've got great news! Mr. Ang wants to go forward with the merger."

The knot in Brian's stomach felt like a brick now.

"Melinda's gone."

"What?"

"Melinda's gone. She was on the flight to Brazil that they can't find. She's dead Chuck. She's dead."

Chuck sat in the chair across from him.

"Jesus. I'm sorry. Are you sure?"

"Well, I wasn't sure of the flight and timing until I found her confirmation ticket. She was on that flight."

"Hold on to some hope, Brian. There's still hope. I tell you what, I can handle the merger from here. All our supporting documents are up to speed. If you're okay with it, I can sign and finish the deal."

"Yeah, Chuck. Thanks."

His phone rang, it was his mom. "Hi Mom."

"Hi Honey, I have good news." She didn't say anything about being hung up on earlier. "Jerry is out of intensive care. We're lucky. He still has partial paralysis on his left side and he's having a hard time speaking. The doctors say that's normal. He's stable and that's all that's important."

"Melinda's dead."

"What?"

"She was on the flight to Brazil that they can't find. She's dead Mom."

"God, Brian, I'm sorry. Can you come out to see Jerry?"

Brian hesitated, struck by the insensitivity of his mom. Of everything actually.

"I'll try," and he hung up the phone.

He went home, poured himself some bourbon and turned on CNN. They still were unable to locate the plane and he's heard nothing from the airline. Nothing. He went upstairs, took a sleeping pill and went to bed. He was still crying when he fell asleep.

The sinking ship dream started again, only this time it was on a loop. It would stop at him drowning then start again. Over and over and over again.

He had the awareness to ask himself:

Am I missing something? Why is this repeating? Was it trying to tell me something?

Each time: Waking up to the Deep Insight as a boy, his dad working and his mom being proud. Then, heavy seas and he drowns. Rinse, repeat. Rinse, repeat. Rinse. Repeat.

Water. Sea water. The dream stopped and he woke up, gasping for air. He felt the sudden urge to get to sea water. He threw on some clothes, fired up his Range Rover and headed for Ballard. There was a marina there, right on Puget Sound.

He arrived around 3:00 in the morning. The park was closed so he pulled off the main road and parked in the marina parking lot. As he got out of the car, the smell almost made him throw up. It was the same smell from his dream.

He took a deep breath and started heading for the water. He worked his way north, climbing over several fences and managed to get to the beach. As he was walking he doubled over in pain, crying, as his heart continued to open and break. Another wave came, doubling his knees and bringing him to the ground. After he regained himself, he looked up to find the old man in the fedora sitting on a park bench. He stumbled to him and sat down.

"Everything happens for a reason, Brian. The only time things repeat themselves is when we haven't listened – we haven't uncovered what life is trying to tell us. These patterns repeat themselves, even if we numb ourselves out.

"The listener is the key. It's like a piano cord being struck. If there's no one there to hear it, it plays anyway. Different though, is that in this case, if the piano cord is struck and someone does hear it, it plays more and more cords until a symphony is created.

"Listen to your life, Brian. Listen."

The old man walked off.

"Listen to what?" Brian yelled. "My wife is dead, my father almost died, I could go to jail for falsifying documents and I keep drowning in a stupid ship! Listen to what!!?"

It was then that it struck him. Listen to his dreams. The sinking ship, the retirement home and his wife having an affair.

Listen.

Holy shit. Which one?

Deep Insight, sinking ship, sea water.

Brian came to in his bed, his empty flask in his right hand. His mouth tasted like dried wax paper and his head hurt. He staggered into the bathroom and got in the shower.

Man, that water feels good.

Water. Was he dreaming? Maybe all of this is a dream. That's got to be it.

His alarm went off broadcasting the daily news: "And there is no verification of death as of yet on flight BA716 from Atlanta…. Authorities are still scouring the ocean for signs of life and debris. In other news…"

Brian's heart sank. He showered amidst his crying. The tears seemed to blend in with the shower water creating a never ending stream. The doorbell rang. He quickly toweled off and threw on some clothes.

It was the airline.

"Hello Mr. Richardson, my name is Carl Jacobs, I'm with the airlines. May I come in?"

Brian opened the door as the young black man took a seat in the living room.

Where was that flask?

"It is with deep regret that I'm here today. It's about your wife, Melinda. We have recovered debris from your wife's flight. As of yet, we have been unable to recover her personally, but presume she perished in the crash. I'm sorry."

"I'll be right back." Brian blindly headed up the stairs to find his father's flask. It was empty. He walked down stairs, blank, and went to the liquor cabinet. He filled the flask, took a pull and braced himself on the counter as he started to sob uncontrollably. It was as if all of his life's grief was coming out at once. He flashed over a myriad of mistakes he had made, so many regrets and how much he loved her. It was a mixture of grief, agony and pain. All at once.

He walked out to the living room, thanked the man and asked him to leave.

"Do you have someone you can call, Mr. Richardson? Now isn't a good time to be alone."

"Yes I do, thank you," and he escorted the young man out.

This isn't happening. None of this is happening.

His cell phone started ringing. There were calls coming in from friends and family all over the United States. They must have announced her name over the news.

Great, he thought. *Just great.*

He needed to get away. The urge to leave, to run, to get away from everything welled up in him. He threw some clothes in his gym bag, grabbed his wallet, phone, car keys and flask and headed to his car.

He was leaving and he didn't know where he was going.

This all had to be a dream. It had to be.

Around 11:00 a.m. he was on I-5 passing through Vancouver, Washington when his phone rang. It was Chuck.

"Man, I'm sorry," he said. "I don't know what to say and I'm a bit torn up with how to handle this. I have some good news though. Mr. Ang has decided to move forward ahead of schedule. His board has signed the paper work. It's official. We're rich, Brian. We're rich!"

There was no longer a knot in his stomach, it was now an empty space. A dark space void of any substance. The sound of "We're rich" rattled around inside him as if to echo the words and make it more real. He'd never felt more alone in his life.

Several hours later, he found a small hotel just outside of Eugene. It was nothing fancy, but it was clean. He decided to crash here for the night. He unlocked the door of room number 17 and threw his bag on the floor. He took a pull from his flask and tossed himself backwards on the bed. The crying started again. It swelled from within him. With each breath his lungs heated up to the point they felt like they were burning. His chest hurt, right beneath his sternum. It wasn't a heart attack, but something significant was happening. Each time he took a breath it felt as if his heart was breaking - like a piece of blown glass taken beyond its limits. His heart was breaking, from the inside out. He took more deep breaths as his heart ached and broke.

He was coming back to life.

He saw the dream again, the one where he was eight. The truth was, his mom and stepdad never really got along. His stepdad, Jerry, was always about work. "Work hard and a man can achieve anything!" That was his mantra and he lived it every day. It cost him his relationship with Brian, though. He never knew his real dad, at least not that he could remember. Jerry was a figure head, someone he could point to at school and say he had a dad, but really didn't.

The pain in his chest eased up a bit as he put a hand to his chest and he grabbed a towel to wipe the sweat from his face.

Am I going nuts? he thought. *What is going on?*

He decided to call his mom and find out how Jerry was doing. It rang and rang, no one answered.

He was hungry and decided to venture out for food. He opened the door and noticed a lot had changed. Everything actually.

The car parked in front of his door was a 1957 Chevy Bel Air and it was in mint condition, so was the 1959 Ford Fairlane next to it.

"What the…"

All the cars were from a different era. They were from the fifties and sixties, and they were all like new. He suddenly felt very, very, uneasy.

He went to the office and talked to the clerk. She recognized him from the night before. "Hello, Mr. Richardson, how are you today?" Her clothes were vintage.

A man walked into the hotel. As the door opened, it bumped against the small bell hanging just above it. Brian took a quick look, then felt the knot in his stomach. He looked again. It was his father, James. His biological father, James that left him when he was two.

Sweat started pouring from his forehead and he reached for a deep breath. He only found a shallow one. He stepped to the side to give him room. James told the clerk he was heading to Seattle from Los Angeles and needed a room for the night. As he was filling out the hotel sheet, he glanced up and looked at Brian.

"Hi."

"Hello," Brian said. "To Seattle, huh? I hear it's a wonderful place up there."

He was going to ask if he was heading to Microsoft, then he remembered his frame of reference was sixty years out of date. "Are you heading up to work for Boeing?"

"No," said James. "I'm feeling the urge to move up there. I was there a few years ago and it felt like home. I decided to follow through and listen."

Listen. Listen.

"Say, I was just heading out for some food, may I buy you a cup of coffee?"

"Sure," said James. "Let me get settled in the room, say twenty minutes."

"Sounds great. I'll see you then."

With a smile, James took his bag and headed to his room on the floor above Brian's.

This is interesting, Brian thought. *Really interesting.*

He reached for the flask on the table and it was gone.

Twenty minutes later, James walked through the door, ringing the bell again as he did.

"You ready?"

"Sure," said Brian, "let's go."

They walked down the main street to a little diner. Everywhere, there were cars from the early to late fifties and early sixties. The women were dressed in vibrant clothes, wore hats and the men sported fedoras and pressed colorful plaid shirts. The air was crisp and clean and there was a sense of a slower pace in the air. Brian felt at home.

They found a cozy spot by the window. It was a large booth with a little jukebox on the wall.

Nice, thought Brian. *Nice.*

"What brings you to Eugene?" asked James. Brian stammered for a minute, he wasn't sure what to say.

"I felt the need to get away, to clear my head and this was the first stop along the way."

"Ah," said James. "Where are you from?"

"Seattle," replied Brian. "Seattle."

"Interesting," James said. "I'd love to hear more about it. How long have you lived there?"

"Since I was seven. I was born in LA and my mom and I moved up there, then. That's when my mom met my stepdad and they got married. So, it's been a while."

"Interesting," said James. They talked for several minutes, ordered their food and ate. Brian couldn't help but wonder if James had put the pieces together.

I guess it doesn't matter, he thought. *Why is he here?*

"Listen," the old man had said.

Listen.

"So, the money dried up for me in LA. I was in a lucrative business, selling cars. One thing led to another and I lost everything. It's time to make a change, I thought. Time for a change. I'm looking forward to it actually."

"How did you end up in sales?" Brian asked.

"I've always had a knack for it. I have my own unique approach. Rather than trying to sell something to someone, like my boss wants, I find out what they want and get it for them. I don't let my boss know this because sometimes I send the customer to our competitor.

To me, 'selling' something to someone is, well, unhealthy."

"How did you come to learn this?" Brian asked. "It's a pretty unusual approach."

"I learned it at the school of hard knocks. I tried the 'Sell, Sell, Sell' idea, hitting quotas and pushing people. I became successful at it really quick. Within the first quarter I took home the "top dog" award for our dealership and then it happened."

"What's that?"

"Well," James looked down at his coffee. "I'll tell you another time. Suffice it to say, I learned the hard way that cheating other people to get ahead haunts you. It's like everything from that moment on is tainted. Things from that point on don't smell, feel or seem the same. It's like bad milk or something. It didn't work for me."

It was obvious James was getting uncomfortable so Brian changed the subject.

"Are you a Dodgers fan?"

"You bet! I grew up in New York and when they came to LA, I thought, 'Hot Damn! They're following me.'" Both of them chuckled for a minute as their conversation turned to Gil Hodges, Don Drysdale and Sandy Koufax. They laughed, talked, had some ice cream and called it a night.

As they walked back to the hotel, James told him: "I'm feeling compelled to tell you - trust your gut Brian. It's never failed me. Trust your gut."

With a firm and long handshake, they said their good byes. Brian went to his room, went inside and flopped down on his bed. He woke up in the same position, scared and disoriented.

Where am I? Wait, when am I?

He took a deep breath and reached for the flask on the table. It was gone.

What is going on?!

"Listen," he heard a soft voice say. "Listen."

6

He pulled back the drapes and looked outside. The cars were back to normal.

Good, he thought. *Good.*

He showered, shampooed, shaved and packed. As he was heading out the door, a twinge showed up in his stomach. It was a small one, but still noticeable.

He hopped into his Range Rover and headed south again on I-5. Now, he knew where he was going, Sacramento. Home.

That afternoon, he pulled up to his childhood home, a one story stucco rambler, LA style. The memories flooded back in, some good, some not so good. He choked down the "not so good" ones and rang the doorbell.

"Brian!" his mom screamed, "I'm so glad you're here. Where have you been? I've been worried sick!" Immediately, all the memories of that phrase came flooding in. Three years old, four years old... hundreds upon hundreds of times. Words like, "How could you?" or "What were you thinking," or "Don't you know how that makes me feel," along with "You're such a good boy."

It dawned on him. It was like he was a puppy being trained how to be. He lost himself when he learned to take care of his mom's feelings. "Keep listening" he heard. "Keep listening."

"Don't just stand there, come in!" she chortled. "Can I pour you a drink?" More memories now. He had forgotten how much liquor was a part of his mom's and Jerry's life. They drank at every meal and off and on throughout the day. The knot in his stomach started talking to him. It ached.

"Well," she began, "I'll have you know Jerry is going to be fine, thank you. You could have tried to call or told me you were coming Brian. Really."

A small pang of guilt started to swell in him. Then, it occurred to him that she was so involved in her own world that she had forgotten that Melinda had died. It was as if things that weren't happening to her directly didn't actually happen.

"So, how is the merger coming?" she asked. Knot again. Knot again. "It's coming along fine. Actually, better than fine. Our parent company signed the paperwork yesterday, so it will be finalized in a day or so."

"That's great," she said. "How's...?" she stopped. "I'm sorry Brian. How are you? I know things must be hard for you."

"I'm doing okay Mom, I'm doing okay." She took a large pull from her wine glass and Brian became glad he couldn't find the flask any more.

She went on to talk about how Jerry was doing, how the doctors worked to save him and gave him a rundown of his condition, from head to toe.

"Do you want to come see him with me this evening?"

"Sure mom, I'd be glad to."

"He isn't talking well yet..." she paused. "I told him I'd be there at 5:30. Do you want to go to your room and unpack?"

Go to your room, go to your room.

More memories. Memories of going to his room to, "Think about what you've done," which really meant: Figure out what she wanted to hear, and say it, so you can come out. It was nerve-racking, frustrating and crazy making all at once. It never really mattered what he thought, it was all about his mom, what she thought, what her feelings were - and his job was to make her happy.

He went to his rig, got his bags and cell phone and noticed he had a text from Chuck.

"It's done man, its done! We're rich!"

Knot in stomach the size of a loaf of bread, thank you. He sighed, started to cry, then turned the tears off like water from a bathroom faucet. He took his bags and went up to his room. He opened the door and saw that nothing had changed. His old posters were still up, his baseball trophies and his soap box derby trophy were all exactly where they were, eleven years ago when he left. They were all clean, dusted and like nothing had changed.

He flopped down on the bed and gazed at the ceiling.

What happened? he thought. *I was so happy as a kid.*

Things were going so well, what happened? What happened?

A bell rang. Suddenly the memory of him playing doctor flooded in.

"How could you think of doing such a thing?" his mom asked. "You know that's not what you really want to do. Jerry said there's tons of money to be made in computers. You just have to think ahead. He says: 'Work hard and a man can achieve anything.' You'll be a fine entrepreneur someday. A fine one Brian. You'll be rich and you can retire when you're thirty. Mommy is so proud of you. I'm so happy."

Tears started rolling down Brian's face. Years of backed up tears. Ones for every time he was told he was wrong, shouldn't think this way or that, and told what he really wanted to do in life. Tears for, "That's a silly idea" and "How could you after all I've done for you?" Tears mixed in with pain, a heart breaking open and one of the many knots in his stomach getting smaller. His chest ached again, deeply.

"Briiii aan! Are you ready?"

"Sure Mom, I'll be right down." He washed his face, cleared his head and headed down the stairs.

What's next?

They got to the hospital and arrived in Jerry's room right on time, as usual. Right on time.

Jerry didn't look well. He was pale and had lost so much weight. It looked like he was ready to give up. Jennifer walked to the other side of the bed and sat in the chair next to him. Brian inched closer and just then, Jerry opened his eyes. He had a shocked look on his face and his brown eyes were as intense as he's ever seen.

"Brrr iii annn?" he asked.

"Yes dad, I'm here."

He took a slow breath and said, "I'm sorry."

"Sorry for?"

"Sorry for not being there for you. Sorry for not listening to what you were really saying. Sorry for working so much and not being a good dad for you."

As Jerry was saying the words, Brian noticed his speech wasn't slurred. Not one bit. It was clear as a bell. He looked over at his mom and she was in her own little world, gazing out the window. She was oblivious to what was being said... she didn't hear a word.

"What do you mean, Dad? You were there. You provided for me."

"I wasn't there to stand up for you against your mom. She means well, but I knew what she was doing to you and, well, I never stepped in. I was miserable and hated myself. I'm sorry."

Tears welled up in Brian's eyes. He was finally being seen, being seen for who he really was. For the first time in his life, he felt like someone was there for him, with no strings. He felt seen, validated and noticed. Then the anger started.

No, not now. Tonight.

Right as Jerry said he was sorry, the look in his eyes faded. He went back to looking frail and weak with a glazed look in his eyes. He looked once again, like a man that had a stroke and was waiting to die.

"Mom, I need to go," Brian said.

"Humm?" she murmured as she pulled herself out of the far away trance she was in. "Okay sweetie. Whatever you want. That's fine."

He caught a taxi back home.

He awoke the next morning to find a text on his phone from Melinda.

"Babe, we need to talk."

Oh my god, she's alive. She's alive!

He switched to phone mode and called her.

"Hello."

"Hi Babe, my God, you're alive. I'm so grateful. What happened?"

"That's what I need to talk with you about Brian. I'm in Utah, at my mom's. Can you come here?"

"What's going on? I don't understand." Yet another knot formed in his stomach.

"I don't want to go over this on the phone. What do you say?"

"Okay. I can be there in a couple of days, one maybe. Does that work for you?"

"Yes, that works. Call me when you get in town."

"Okay. I love…." She had hung up.

The next morning, Brian set out for Utah, perplexed, stressed and confused.

7

He knew what James and Jerry had told him was significant, but he couldn't put his finger on why. He was actually amazed that these experiences weren't freaking him out more. It all seemed a bit surreal, frankly. The past few days he was having a hard time telling where and when he was. It was a bit unsettling.

He went to a gas station to fill up, and right as he got out of his car, his phone blew up. There must have been thirty-five to forty calls and fifty or so texts in the span of thirty seconds.

What the heck, he thought.

As he got out of the car, he started putting fuel into his rig and the automated marketing feature of the pump started filling him in on the day's news.

"In other news, Mobile Tech Web Solutions and Ang & Tanaka incorporated have merged in an unprecedented and much anticipated approach. Brian Richardson and his partner Chuck Hamilton are now some of the richest tech men in the United States."

The knot formed in his stomach as they flashed his and Chuck's picture on the screen. Sweat started forming as he imagined his office full of FBI agents with search warrants. He found himself in a small room with an inmate named Frederick who had done time for money laundering for a Columbian cartel. He started to get nauseous. A car honk brought him back to the present.

He tugged off the receipt, got in his car and keyed in his wife's parent's address into his GPS. He was off to Logan, Utah.

A couple of hours later, he was driving through Reno. Something told him to stop off for a few minutes and grab some food. There was a small diner on the end of town that looked enticing. It was in the shape of an old train caboose. "Frank's Diner," it said.

Sounds good.

He went in, sat down and looked over the menu.

Biscuits and gravy, nice.

He hadn't had them in years. He was greeted by a nice looking blonde waitress named Peggy.

"How are you, Darlin'?"

"I'm great thanks. May I get your biscuits and gravy?"

"Sure thing. They'll be right up."

As she walked off he heard the distinct click, click, click sound. It was almost like the sound when you put a baseball card on your bike so it flutters in the spokes.

Click. Click. Click. Click. Now he heard what sounded like a rock skipping on the ground and slowly coming to a stop.

Now what?

Inexplicably, he had a wave of happiness come over him.

A few minutes passed and Brian realized he wasn't actually thinking about anything.

Interesting, he thought.

Peggy brought his biscuits, gravy and an orange juice.

"Thank you, but I didn't order the orange juice."

"No worries Darlin'. It's on the house," and she set the meal down in front of him.

He took his first bite and another wave of happiness came over him. He couldn't quite put his finger on why, he just knew he felt happy, deep down inside. He polished off his meal, took the last bite of biscuit and circled the plate with it, soaking up what was left of the gravy. He put it in his mouth, swallowed and with a sense of satisfaction he hadn't felt in years, smiled from the inside out. He walked to the cashier counter and paid.

"Thank you. That was the best meal I've had in years."

"Glad to hear it Darlin', glad to hear it."

He left a generous tip and headed out of the diner.

The best meal he's had in years…

Back on I-80, he picked up his journey. Two hours in, he got a call from Chuck Hamilton. He tapped the "accept" button on his car's computer screen and Chuck chimed in: "How does it feel to be so rich? Man, can you believe it? We can retire. I can retire… All that work paid off baby! Woo hoo! I'm stoked. I've got my eye on a Porsche Targa, gonna go test drive it this afternoon."

Then there was a brief pause.

"Sorry Brian, I forgot you've got other things going on. How the hell are you? I've only got a few minutes, so you know."

So much had happened to Brian in the last eight days, he didn't know where to start. He also thought Chuck would think he was a bit loopy if he told him, so he decided to keep it surface. "I'm good," Brian said. "I found out that Melinda is alive."

"What?" he said. "Seriously! I'm so glad. Wait, what the hell? Why didn't she call you? Excuse me…." He heard the sound of the phone being muffled. "I'll get with them in a few minutes. Tell them I'll call right back and no, I'm not available for interviews today."

"Sorry Brian, things are a bit chaotic here, well, you get that I'm sure. Where was I?"

"I'm not sure why she didn't. I'm heading to her mom's to see her…she called me from there yesterday. She wouldn't say why she was there or what was going on. It doesn't feel good, I can tell you that."

"Well, I'm here for you buddy. Just let me know how I can help." There was an awkward pause. "I gotta go. Talk soon?"

"Ok, sure Chuck."

"Bye."

Brian clicked the phone off and heard a heavy sigh come out of his mouth.

Several hours passed and he needed to take a pit stop, "duty calls."

He pulled into the next rest stop, hopped out and stretched a bit. He went to the men's room, took care of things, walked out and was suddenly struck by the beauty of the area around him. He walked across the grass and took a deep breath of the fresh mountain air.

What a screwed week. I can't believe this. Everything is falling apart.

Everything I ever wanted is falling apart.

Suddenly, he became aware of his feet on the ground. A wave of warmth came up through the grass and he started to feel at peace again. A car pulled up and parked. When the door opened he heard a familiar song and a memory started pouring in.

He was instantly seven.

"But I want to," he was pleading to his mom.

"You know you can't do that. We've never done anything like it and frankly, we can't afford it. Besides, what will other people think?" The crying started again, from deep down. He realized how he had given up on his dream...on himself.

He made it back to his rig and sat inside. After several minutes, the waves of emotions subsided. He started back on I-80. After a couple of hours, he realized he knew he couldn't go through with forging the documents for his company, it flat out felt off. He "auto called" Chuck.

Chuck picked up.

"Chuck, it's Brian. I can't do this. If they find out about the documents, we'll end up in prison."

"Brian, shut up. They won't find out. Only you and I know."

"I don't care. I can't live with myself. It doesn't feel right."

"Who are you, Brian? What's up all of a sudden with your conscience? Where the hell did that come from? You've wanted to retire ever since I've known you. It was the reason we started this business in the first place. Now, we get it and it 'doesn't feel right.' What's the matter with you? People would kill to be in the position you are, Brian."

He hung up.

Brian pulled over, stopped and started to cry. From the bottom of his heart, he started crying. The sobs were so deep, he felt it all over his body. His heart ached and the knot in his stomach just won't go away.

The phone rings, it's his mom.

"He's gone Brian. He's gone. I need you to come home. Come home, Brian."

It felt as if a three-foot hook had just dug itself deep, deep past his sternum and wedged itself there. The pull was tremendous. "Come home, Brian. Come home." The pull became more and more intense, it was like a semi was pulling him. It hurt.

"Mom, I can't right now. I'm on my way to see Melinda. She's alive."

"Well, if that's more important to you, I understand."

The pull changed now to a feeling of shame, disgust and guilt.

"It's not like I haven't been there for you before. Go ahead, take care of yourself Brian. I'll be here when you're done. I always am."

"Good bye, Mom."

"Good bye."

A wave of nausea started in his stomach and radiated out all over his body. "After all I've done for you," rang in his ears. "After all I've done for you."

Brian came to about thirty miles outside of Logan. The sudden scream of "What am I doing!?!" came from the core of his being. He pulled over in a panic. He threw the Range Rover into park and pounded the steering wheel with both hands.

"What the hell is going on??!!" he screamed.

The knot in his stomach was like a brick now, and his heart hadn't stopped hurting. He felt like a plane flying without a compass at night. No lights, no horizon, nothing. It was a horrible feeling.

He took a few deep breaths and managed to regain his composure.

Ok. What is the next step here? What is the next step?

A few more breaths.

Breathe. Breathe.

Next, I go talk with Melinda and pray that:

> *1.) Cops don't come and take me to jail, and*
>
> *2.) My mom doesn't call, and*
>
> *3.) The code I wrote actually works*

He found himself at the Robert's home around 11:30 p.m. and pulled up to the security gate. He rang the buzzer.

"Hello?" It was Melinda's Dad.

"Hi, Mr. Roberts, it's Brian. I'm sorry it's so late.   I'm here to see Melinda."

"Come in," barked the speaker.

The black ornate gate parted in the middle and opened the path to their home. He drove up the driveway and realized he had forgotten the enormity of their place. There were trees on either side of the drive along with a two-foot wide white gravel border framing the black asphalt. He looked ahead to see the pale yellow glow from the windows of the white colonial style mansion - the same mansion he had put out of his memory. He pulled past their six-car garage and parked in front of their entrance way. His heart sank deep, past his chest and felt heavy in his gut.

The billionaire Roberts' home. Great.

He took a deep breath and walked up the three steps made out of off white brick. The solid oak door was bathed in the soft white light of the chandelier that hung above. He rang the doorbell and waited.

Mr. Roberts opened the door.

"Hi, Brian. Come on in. Melinda's upstairs. She'll be down in a minute. Shall we wait for her in the living room?"

"Sure, Mr. Roberts. Sure."

Brian walked through the entranceway and turned left where he was met by a large sitting area lavishly furnished and impeccably clean.

"Thank you," Brian said.

"No problem. Would you like a drink?"

"Sur..." Brian stopped in mid-sentence.

Where is this coming from?

"Uh, no thank you Mr. Roberts, I'm good."

"Okay, more for me," Mr. Roberts chuckled as he poured himself three fingers of bourbon. "Have a seat."

Brian sat at the edge of the flowered white sofa.

Mr. Roberts looked at Brian over the top of his crystal glass. "So I hear you're a rich man, Brian. Congratulations. Quite a few people are talking about it. I'm sure your folks are very proud."

"Thank you, Mr. Roberts. It's true, it became final yesterday. The merger went through and all is good. I'm bit fuzzy about the whole thing actually."

"Well, I remember when I first met you, I had my doubts." He took a pull off his bourbon. "You may have money now, but..."

Melinda appeared out of the corner of Brian's eye. His heart leapt and sank in an instant.

She is so beautiful, he thought. *So beautiful.*

"Hi Brian," she said. "Dad, may we have a minute?"

"Sure, Doll, I'll be in the den if you need me."

Need me? Need me? thought Brian.

Brian realized he felt an enormous weight in the room. There was something almost palpable between Melinda and him. He wanted to walk over, hug and kiss her but that presence was keeping him from it.

Melinda sat on the loveseat directly across from him. "I thought you were dead," Brian said. "God, I thought you were dead."

"I'm sorry I didn't call, Brian. I needed some time."

"Time for?"

"This wasn't a business trip, Brian. I was going to spend time with Chuck."

"What?" The energy in Brian's body escalated to a barely controllable level.

"My Chuck? I mean... Chuck?"

"Yes, we were going to spend some time together. I backed out, I got off at the last minute in Atlanta. I couldn't do it."

Brian's throat was dry and his tongue felt thick and sticky. He was in shock.

"I don't understand Melinda. What did I do? I was a good husband. We spent time together, I treated you right. I love you Melinda. What the...?"

"I'm not sure," she interrupted. "I've given it a lot of thought. Over the past several years, you've changed, Brian. You're different than the man I married, than the man I fell in love with."

"What do you mean?" he asked. It felt like he was observing himself saying things now. It was as if he was no longer present in his body.

"I finally hit it big... WE finally hit it big! Melinda, the merger went through yesterday."

"I know, I heard. It doesn't matter to me Brian. Money doesn't matter to me."

"That's because you have all this. Of course money wouldn't matter. You don't need it. You never have 'needed' it. Now I have it and you're leaving. Right when I made it, you're leaving?"

"I'm sorry, Brian."

The room became eerily quiet. All Brian noticed was the subtle clicking of an antique clock marking the time that was going by. It occurred to him how loud it really was. Tick. Tock. Tick. Tock.

There was so much more to cover, so many questions, he had hundreds, yet he realized the conversation was done for tonight.

He felt like he was back in his body again.

"Okay, Melinda, okay." Brian left, dazed, confused and mostly numb.

8

It was around 1:30 a.m. when he flopped face first on the reasonably warn bedspread of the nearby motel.

Good enough for tonight, he thought. *Good enough for tonight.*

He was awakened at 2:45 by himself. He was talking to himself while he was dreaming.

"How could you do this?" he shouted.

"What did I do exactly?!!? If she wasn't so rich this would have worked. If she hadn't lied and just stayed home everything would be okay. Chuck. Chuck, you bastard!"

He went to the bathroom and splashed cold water on his face.

At least it wasn't the dreams.

They would come later.

He woke up at 6:45 a.m. in a cold sweat, realizing part of his dreams were coming true. Melinda was having an affair. It was in that moment he decided to look into these dreams more. He wasn't sure how yet, but he had a feeling that they were the most important dreams he'd ever had.

He showered, shampooed and shaved. As he was raking a comb across his thick black hair, he began to think about what the old man in the fedora had said to him.

"Listen. Listen to your life," he'd said.

Well, there was quite a bit to listen to. His stepdad passing, the merger, his wife having an affair and the possibility of going to jail for fraud. What was his life trying to tell him?

With this question in his mind, he realized he was hungry and went out looking for a place to eat. He ended up at a place called "Beth's," a quaint little dinner in the heart of downtown Logan.

As he opened the door, the comforting smell of freshly brewed coffee mingled in the air. He took a long sniff.

Ahhh. That brings back memories.

As he was being seated he remembered the mornings with his dad, Jerry, and he started to tear up. His mom would have a fresh pot of coffee going made from the Mr. Coffee she had bought him for Christmas. Dad had fixed omelets for everyone with fresh bacon, chives and cheddar cheese - his favorite. They sat down at the flowery yellow Formica table fresh out of the sixties. You see, they didn't have much back then, but they were happy. A family with a deep, loving connection.

Dad set down his breakfast, which was on a yellow patterned Corelle plate. Brian was ready to eat. Mom and Dad sat down and they talked about how each was doing. Mom said things were going better, her Tupperware parties were starting to take hold. Dad mentioned he was looking forward to a promotion and hoping he could actually work less hours in the process. Brian was a bit perplexed, he had a huge appetite yet something was troubling him.

"I'm getting picked on at school. I don't like it there," he blurted. "Everyone says I'm different. I'm scared. I don't want to go any more."

"Brian, that is so not okay," his dad remarked. "Who is doing this? Tell us all about it."

He shared how the kids were calling him weird, how they picked on him because he was cute and even called him "gay." He talked about how he was having a hard time talking in front of his classmates now, and that he'd been hit more than a couple of times by two boys, Mike and Thomas.

His mom piped in. "Brian, I'm so glad you're telling us this. This isn't about you. You're an amazing boy and I'm angry those boys are treating you this way. I'm glad because you don't need to handle these things alone, that's our job, to keep you safe. Jerry, would you be able to go to school with me this week to talk to his principal."

"I think I can make some time this Friday, would that work, Hon?"

"Yes."

"In the meantime, I'm going to call your teacher, Miss Thompson and let her know," she said.

"Please don't," chimed Brian. "The kids will find out and it will get worse."

"Brian," his mom said in a loving voice. "This is our job, to take care of you."

"Don't worry, Son," Jerry said. "We'll take care of you."

Brian realized tears were streaming down his face. He reached down, grabbed a napkin and wiped his tears away. Another puff in the napkin cleared his nose.

What the heck, Brian thought.

The stuff with the kids was true, the problems at school and getting beat up, also true. His parents never talked to him like that though... ever. Something weird was going on. It felt so real, like it actually happened. He wished it had really been like that. Really.

Just then, Brian looked up to see the old man in the familiar fedora walking his way. He was whistling the same song as last time. He came to his booth and asked, "May I sit down, Son? I may be of service."

Brian felt the warmth and compassion the old man had about him.

"Sure," he said, "But be nice. It's been a rough week."

Just then, Brian's order arrived. A bacon, cheese and chive omelet.

Interesting, he thought. *Interesting.*

He dug in and the old man started.

"How are you, Son?"

"I've been better. Over the course of nine days my stepdad has died, I'm seeing how mean my mother is, I found out my wife is having an affair, I'm having these weird dreams and ... oh, and, I'm a multi-millionaire."

"Well, it doesn't sound all bad."

"The millionaire part comes with strings - it wasn't honest."

"Oh. I meant everything, Brian. Everything. You see, with time and perspective, the worst things that happen to us often turn into the best things."

This guy is nuts. Flat out nuts!

"You have never experienced any of this, old man."

"Actually, I have. I was born in the Great Depression. I grew up in a burg in Brooklyn. We were starving Brian, starving, but somehow we managed to survive. I had the gift of a father that had a very unique look on life. He used to always say, 'Son, something good will come out of this. You just wait and see.' I'll be darned if he wasn't right. It took patience, faith, inner strength and persistence. He was right, Brian, he was right.

"My first wife left me for my best friend. I was devastated. I thought it was me, that I had done something wrong, that I wasn't a good enough husband. It wasn't true, you see, it was about her choices, not mine. I remember vividly hearing my dad's voice, 'Something good will come out of this, Son. Trust me.'

"Sure enough, with time, I realized I wasn't happy in my marriage with Belinda. I was so involved in how things looked that I didn't even notice. Her running off was the best thing that ever happened to me. It helped me get that we weren't a fit and I was able to see my part in it, too. I gave myself credit for keeping my heart open to the best of my ability. I think, deep down, I knew we weren't meant to be.

"Then, four years later I met Wanda - the love of my life. It was so easy with her. We became deep friends so quickly. We laughed, supported each other and I loved her deeper than I ever did Belinda.

"In a way," he chuckled, "her leaving was to make me happy."

"Do you see, Brian?"

His stomach had back flipped several times by now. "Are you saying that Melinda's affair is a good thing?"

"I'm saying, with perspective, it may be. Also, don't jump to conclusions. Our brains want to make the worst of things, have you noticed?"

"No, they seem to be there to protect us. As I figure out all the strategies of how to deal with things, of how to cope, it helps me know what to do. It's my friend."

"Well, Brian, consider that sometimes it's your worst enemy. Your heart on the other hand…"

"May I ask you a question?"

"Besides that one?" the old man asked with a grin.

"Sure. Why not?"

"What do you know about the affair?"

"Everything," he said angrily. "That she was having it with my business partner, Chuck, that they were heading to Belize to spend time together and that I had changed."

"But, what do you really know?"

"What do you mean?"

"Think about asking her specifically what happened between them. Our brains have a tendency to leap to the worst. Oftentimes, it isn't. Also, you might consider asking her, specifically, what's changed in you.

"If you're afraid, gather the information. It's a great way to keep yourself - your brain - from going to the worst.

"Do you feel the fear of your wife leaving?"

"Yes."

"Then ask the questions, especially if you're afraid of the answer. That way you'll have the information that will help you make your decision."

"I have to run," the old man said. "I'm on a schedule." With a wink and a tap of his cap, the old man slid out of the booth and headed out of the diner.

What a trippy week, Brian thought. *What a trippy week.*

9

He decided to call Melinda and see if they could talk somewhere. He didn't want to go to her house, he realized how intimidated he was with all their money.

They met at a small park with a beautiful little pond in the center. They sat together on an old park bench, one at each end. The distance between them was apparent, physically and otherwise.

"Thanks for meeting with me, Melinda."

"Sure, Brian. Sure."

"It wasn't all bad, was it?" he asked.

"No, Brian, it wasn't." He felt a knot in his stomach.

"I want to know about your affair. I don't need all the details, just the specifics."

"Ok."

"How long?"

"Not long. We'd been getting together for lunch here and there for a few months. It actually started before that, though. Brian, he would listen to me. He made time for me and he, well, he cared enough to listen."

Brian's heart was thumping in his chest.

He took a deep breath and asked, "Did you...sleep with him?"

"No, Brian. I couldn't. We were supposed to spend the week together in Belize and I'm sure that was part of it. I couldn't go through with it, though. That's why I got off the plane."

Thank God, Brian thought.

"So, you didn't sleep with him? You were going to, but couldn't. Why couldn't you?"

Brian wasn't sure where that question came from, it sounded odd and he wasn't really aware he asked it.

"I love you, Brian. I always have. It just didn't feel right."

Brian's heart began to hurt again, it felt like an egg cracking open from the heat as it was being boiled. Not necessarily a bad thing, it hurt none the less. It ached.

"Something good will come out of this," he heard the old man say. He repeated it to himself. "Something good will come out of this."

"What did you say?" she asked.

"Sorry," he said. He remembered the second question the old man had suggested – what changed in him?

"What did I do? What was my part in this?" he asked.

"I don't know Brian. At some point, you seemed to stop caring," she paused.

"Can I be direct with you?" she asked.

"Absolutely," he heard himself say.

"It was when you started this new company. I knew your heart wasn't in it. You liked the job okay but you were doing it for the money. You even said, 'It'll be for a short amount of time, Melinda.' Then we can retire.

"I remember thinking, I don't want the money. I'd rather spend time with you.

"The second year I saw the stress and pressure take its toll, all the hours and pushing. You tried to control everything and your fears started to grow. Then you started drinking more and talking with me less," she paused. "That's all I have for you at this point. Okay?"

Brian looked at her, she was so beautiful. Suddenly, he realized how blue her eyes were. He had forgotten that. He had been so caught up in her outward appearance that he had forgotten who she really was. As he looked into her eyes, he saw her pain, the ache that was there for her, too. His heart cracked open a bit more.

Brian took a deep breath. "Thank you. I've always appreciated how direct you can be."

"You're welcome. Look, I need to go. This is a lot for me, too. I need to go home, ok?"

"Sure," Brian said. "Sure."

"I love you," he added.

"I love you too, Brian. I always have."

He watched her walk away and realized how empty he felt inside.

Something good will come out of this. Something good will come out of this.

As he sat there it started to dawn on him. She was spot on. Spot on.

Something at the back of his being told him things were starting to come together. He couldn't tell what exactly, it was a feeling.

"Listen," the old man had said, "listen." He began to think of Chuck, the serpent that was chasing his wife. Geez, he was married, too. His phone rang. Guess who? Chuck. He swiped left and let it go to voice mail.

Anger started to swell inside him, and he realized it wouldn't help the situation. He knew he couldn't listen to anything when he was this mad.

Deep breath. Okay, he thought, *listen.*

What had he learned so far?

> His biological dad had said, "Nothing good comes from cheating."

> The old man had said, "Listen."

> He also said, "Something good comes out of everything."

> His stepdad has passed away and right before that, he apologized for not seeing him.

> He was realizing how self-absorbed his mom is.

> He felt intimidated by Melinda's wealth.

> He's a multi-millionaire, but he cheated to get there.

And, those damn dreams.

The penny dropped. The first dream was warning him not to go through with the merger. It was telling him that if he did, he would be in a sinking ship and he would drown and die.

His life told him again when he saw the model for the same ship at the meeting, and he ignored it.

Click.

Okay, he thought. *The next step: Quit the company.*

Wait, something didn't feel right. His stomach was unsettled. "Trust your gut," James had said.

What am I missing? Deep breath.

I need to fix things before I leave. His stomach eased up.

That's it. I need to fix things before I leave. How can I do that?

Brian, realizing how overthinking had created such a mess in his life, decided to just ask the question and sit with it. He'd listen to see what his life said.

What is best for me to do next?

That night, the second dream returned. It started earlier this time and it more real and more palpable. He wound up not knowing where or when he was. He vividly remembered the feeling of being retired and not being with his wife.

That made sense, he thought. *It fits. I need to leave Mobile Tech. I'm on the right track.* He checked in and it felt right to him.

He woke up and decided to go for a jog. He thought it would help both with his nerves and to clean the air between his ears. Besides, he hadn't been on a run in over five years.

Five years! he thought. *That's right, I stopped doing this because of the business.*

Since it had been so long - no running shoes. He went down to the local sporting goods store to pick up a new pair. He found some that were yellow, with a blue stripe. He loved them.

As he was trying them on a store worker came by. "Are you sure you want those? We've got some newer ones out back, they're much less expensive and a better buy. There aren't any yellow ones, but they're a way better deal."

"Sure," Brian said. "Sounds good." He started to unlace the shoes and immediately something felt off. He remembered all the times he had been talked out of what he wanted by his mom, and other people, too. "Get a red one, not yellow," and "Are you sure? People will tease you if you wear that." In class he heard, "Why would you want to write a paper on Gandhi, no one knows who he is. Besides, he was a wimp!" The list was so long and it went on and on and on. He realized the knot was back in his stomach. "Trust your gut, kid," James had said.

"No," blurted Brian. "I'm good. I'll take these."

I love them, he thought.

An unsettling feeling flooded his body. He was uncomfortable, yet he knew he was doing what was right from him. Why was he uncomfortable? They were only a pair of shoes.

His run started off with his long forgotten stretching routine, some brisk walking and a trot.

Man this feels good, he thought. *I feel alive again!*

He started off heading towards the park he had met Melinda at the day before. The air smelled so crisp and clean. He'd forgotten how deep and full his lungs could get with air. After the first mile he started to get a small side ache, so he slowed to a walk.

There are so many things I stopped doing. I stopped running, stopped caring, stopped having fun and stopped listening.

It's time to change things.

He noticed how his heart rang a different note now. It felt full, open and alive. This was new for him, and welcomed.

He started to think about how to fix the paperwork with his company. He needed to make things right with it before he left. As he was walking, he decided to stop thinking. He wanted to give himself an opportunity to have the idea come to him, rather than forcing it. Forcing it, flat out, hadn't worked.

He started to trot gain, enjoying how alive his legs felt, how his body felt, how everything felt. A small Subaru station wagon was coming up behind him. Nothing extraordinary about it, it was light green with a Thule rack on top. As he was jogging he glanced at the bumper. On it was a blue and white bumper sticker that read: "It's never too late to do the right thing."

Click. Then, it occurred to him.

I need to call Mr. Ang.

He felt scared, but his stomach was okay. It was the right thing to do. He knew it.

He finished his run and went back to his room to shower. As he was showering, he let the water run over his back. He focused and paid attention to what he was doing. He realized he wasn't thinking, he was just doing what he was doing, and that was it. He felt the warm water on his back, how his muscles relaxed, how good it felt. He appreciated how the water was refreshing him, how it felt, he was being renewed.

Thank you, he thought. *Thank you.*

As he toweled off, a thought popped into his mind.

How did that coding go for the new client?

It occurred to him that if it went well, it might make up for the money they had forged on their profit and loss statements.

Interesting, Brian thought.

He got dressed, went to the front desk and asked if they had a computer with an internet connection. "Over there," the clerk said. "It's seventy-five cents a minute."

"Sure," Brian said. "Thank you."

He went over and logged on to the antiquated VGA monitor screen. He was half expecting a dial up modem sound. It didn't happen. He logged into his email account from work, there were over 300 emails.

This is what happens when you go away from work for a week, he laughed.

He searched for the email from Tangant Industries, a textile manufacturer prominent in the Seattle supply businesses. They work with home improvement stores and large companies all over the United States. If this worked, it would be worth well over 2.5 million dollars in annual revenue.

He found it.

Bingo!

> "Thank you, Mr. Richardson, for your swift solution to our issues. Your product works wonderfully along with your customization to our unique needs. We are very pleased with your product and would be glad to pay the yearly cost for the rights to use your product and its maintenance. Please call us at your earliest convenience."

"Saweeet!" he blurted out loud as he clapped his hands. He started laughing with joy.

Something good will come out of this. Something good will come out of this!

He found the number for their purchasing agent, called her and arranged to have the paperwork emailed to him for signatures.

Yes!

Brian stopped for a minute and realized how exhausted he was. He made a commitment to himself to take a month off when this was over. He always had dreamed of traveling in Europe.

Patience, he thought. *The paper work will come tomorrow. I'll sign it and once that's done, I'll call Mr. Ang.*

A part of him wanted to rush. His brain was flooded with thoughts of all the steps to take to make things work. This contingency, that contingency. The "What ifs" and the "Then I wills." His head started to buzz and link and spin. Panic started to set in with a blend of anxiety and force. The difference was, this time he saw it. He recognized what his brain was doing.

"Not this time," he said. "Not this time." He took a couple deep breaths.

Patience.

One step at time. Something good will come out of this.

He looked down to see his phone vibrating. It was his mom. He swiped left.

10

He had another dream that night. It was the ship dream. This time, he didn't drown. They all returned to shore safe and sound.

In the morning, he popped in to the motel office and checked his emails. It was there, all the paper work. He printed it out on the dot matrix printer, signed it and went out in search of a copy machine, a post office and breakfast. He hopped into his Range Rover and got this feeling to wait for a minute. He sat in the car trying to figure out what he was missing. He took a deep breath and it occurred to him. His running shoes. He used to run almost every day. He remembered how he loved it, how it brought him peace and joy. He went back to his room, got his shoes, socks, shorts and a towel.

He headed downtown and saw a small "Mom and Pop" drugstore. He pulled in and started to smile. He so liked these little places.

Today's places are so sterile, he thought.

As he walked in he was struck by the eclectic blend of necessities, new technology and sections with knick-knacks, souvenirs and other things you just don't see everywhere.

This place has personality, he mused. *I'll bet the owners are like this, too.*

He asked at the counter if they had a copy machine. "We sure do," the clerk said. "It's in the back on the right side, next to the post office."

"Perfect," Brian said. "Thank you."

He made a couple copies of the legal contract for his business, plopped the original and a copy into the Priority Express envelope, addressed it and handed it to the clerk. "Thank you." he said. "Say, is there a good place to go for a run?" he asked.

"You bet," she said. "There's a five mile run I love to take, it sends you into the mountains a bit and you get a great view of the city, too. Do you have GPS?"

"Sure," he said.

"Plug in 'Brenda's Natural Foods.' The trail starts right behind it."

"Cool. Thanks!"

He was off like a shot. He realized how much he missed his morning runs.

Brenda's parking lot was pretty much empty. True, it was 9:30 in the morning, but still. He parked on the side street, discreetly changed clothes and started his stretching and warm up.

Man, the air here is so fresh. I love it here. I feel so alive.

The trail was clearly marked and it was beautiful. It wove him in and out of trees, up and down some hills, even by a small lake he never knew was there. As he passed the lake on his left, the view of the city appeared. It was beautiful. The sun was part way above it and seemed to set it aglow. He slowed down and stopped.

It struck him how much he had been pushing over the years. Go here, do this, finish that, meet this deadline that deadline, this project, that project. He started to tear up some and felt a twinge in his heart.

I missed so much. So much.

He stood there, hands on his hips for a few minutes, taking in his view, catching his breath… and his insights.

All these insights, dang. It struck him.

"Insight. Deep Insight, like the ship." He laughed out loud. "Well I'll be!" He kept on laughing and started up his run again, with a big grin on his face.

About an hour later he finished up his run and ended up back at his rig.

I've got to do this more often.

He figured he'd give it until tomorrow, then call up Mr. Ang and apologize. He realized his whole "retirement" idea may go south, but frankly, he didn't care. A feeling in the pit of his stomach again.

I wonder what that's about?

On the way back to the motel his phone rang again. It was his mom. This time, he swiped right. "Hi, Mom. How are you?"

"Hi, Brian, when are you coming? Things are a mess here right now. I need you. When are you coming?"

The knot in his stomach was bread loaf sized right now. He took a deep breath. "I'm not going to make it for a few days."

"The funeral is next week, Brian. After all I've done for you the least you can do is be there for me," she said.

"You know he loved you Brian, we both do," and she hung up.

Brian had to pull over. The feelings coming up for him were overwhelming. Anger, fear, rage, guilt, sorrow. It was like a jambalaya of emotions and he didn't know which end was up. He went to reach for this dad's flask.

That's right, no more flask.

He plugged "Liquor store" into his rig's GPS and found one on W. 400th, it wasn't far. He headed there, craving relief from this madness. He started to focus on all the things that had happened wrong in the last few days.

Falsifying documents.

Thinking his wife was dead.

Finding out she was having an emotional affair with his best friend and planned to have sex with him.

His stepdad dying.

Realizing how self-absorbed his mom was.

Having to face Melinda's billionaire dad, and

He was going to jail.

This was too much, too damn much!

He quickly pulled into the liquor store parking lot, threw his car in park and reached for the door handle.

"Trust your gut," James had said.

His gut was telling him something was off.

I'll fix it!

He came out of the liquor store with a fifth of Wild Turkey. He cracked the seal and took a pull as he got into his Range Rover. He fired up his rig and headed back to his hotel.

He parked, went inside and turned on the TV. Live on CNN was an interview with his best buddy, Chuck. He was talking about the merger.

God, he looks pompous, he thought.

A half of a bottle later, he passed out, face down on the bed.

The nightmares returned, all three of them, all in the same way. He sank and drowned in the ship, lost his wife and turned into a class one jerk again.

He woke up hungover, in fear, and realizing that drinking to solve problems wasn't really a solution. He popped six aspirin and went for a walk to clear his head. He ended up at the diner again.

He felt guilty, ashamed and like a failure. He heard the whistling again and wanted to slink into the backrest of his booth. It was the old man in the fedora.

"Hi," he said as he looked at Brian. "You don't look so well, kiddo."

"Funny you mention it, I don't."

"Hitting the sauce, are you?"

"What business is it of yours?"

The old man looked at him. It was as if he knew what Brian was going through.

"Look, Brian. I know things seem hard right now. The problem is your brain, Brian. You see, you've taken on some false beliefs to have the world make sense and to make it harder, you're focusing on what isn't working. You're afraid and your brain is taking over. It's what made the decision to drink again. That's why you don't feel well, Brian. It's your brain.

"What's even more interesting is that we all know what we really want, deep down. The trick is to get out of our own way. Sometimes, fear of the unknown, fear our brain creates, keeps us stuck.

"Your brain can be a friend or an ally. You get to choose. For me, when I'm on the right track, it actually starts to fight. It counters with worry, shame and guilt. If I fight back, it gets worse. I find things to do where I don't think. Find your thing, Brian. Find your thing."

Who the hell is this guy?

"You're probably wondering who I am."

What the…?

"It's not important. Just know that I'm here to help."

"Listen, Brian. Listen. Your life is trying to tell you something. Not your brain… your life. Listen and you'll understand."

The old man left a 'fiver' on the table and headed out, whistling that same song. He almost remembered it. He was close.

Listen?! Listen? That's all I have to do is listen. What kind of mumbo jumbo is that?!

The knot in his stomach seemed to go off like a small bomb and he felt his heart close off. He took a deep breath and looked around him. Another breath.

Calm down, Brian, calm down. Everything is okay. Calm down.

After a few minutes, he felt like his old self. Well, his new old self actually. He realized even more now that he was using liquor to numb the pain. He thought about the third dream, the one on the cruise ship, and remembered how much he was drinking in that dream.

I don't want to turn into that guy. I don't want to put my son through that… wait! I'm going to have a son.

He took another breath and paused.

One step at a time, he thought. *One step at a time.*

He finished his light breakfast and went back to his room.

11

He called Chuck. "Listen, Chuck," he said. "I know you were seeing Melinda. At the least, let's say I'm pissed off at you. That's not why I'm calling though."

Chuck laughed nervously, "Listen Brian," he started.

"I don't care Chuck," he interrupted. "I'm calling to tell you that I solved the problem with the profit and loss statements we lied about. Do you remember the client I coded the new software for, the Tangant Company?

"Yes."

"They've agreed to terms and that's worth 2.5 million annually. That will cover the difference we lied about and more. I'm going to call Mr. Ang as soon as I hang up and come clean."

"Listen, Brian. You can't do that. You'll jeopardize everything. We'll lose everything. Plus, if he reports us…"

"I don't care Chuck, I'm doing it. And then, I'm out. I'm cashing out. I'm done with you and with this whole tech idea." He hung up.

The knot in his stomach was gone and deep down, he knew he was doing the right thing. He called Mr. Ang.

"Mr. Ang please."

"May I ask who's calling?"

"It's Brian Richardson of Mobile Tech."

"One moment."

"Hello, Brian," Mr. Ang said. "How are you?"

"I'm good Mr. Ang, I'm good. I have something to tell you… it's about the merger."

Brian's heart started pounding in his chest. Thump, thump. He knew it was the right thing.

"The initial documents were off. We changed them to make the figures look more enticing. I'm sorry."

There was a short pause. "I understand, Mr. Richardson, and I can't say I'm not disappointed. You realize that this, how do you say, 'inaccuracy,' nullifies our agreement. You could face prison time if I choose to push things, Mr. Richardson."

"Yes, yes I understand, sir."

"While I don't appreciate what you've done, I find your honesty to be courageous. I know it took courage to call me. Is there anything else you wish to tell me?"

"No, Mr. Ang. Wait, sir. There are two things."

"Go ahead."

"First, during our entire merger process we were negotiating with the Tangant Company of North America. We thought it was a long shot so we didn't mention the potential in our meetings..."

"Go on."

"Well, I just signed an agreement with them for five years at 2.5 million dollars a year."

"That's well beyond the numbers you forged."

"Yes sir, it is."

"Is there something else?"

"Yes." He took a breath. "After this situation is settled, in whatever manner it's settled, I'm leaving Micro Tech, sir."

"To do what?"

"I don't know," he paused. "I don't know."

"Thank you Mr. Richardson. I'll be in touch." Mr. Ang hung up.

Brian had an odd feeling going on inside him. It was a mixture of relief, blended in with a sense of doing the right thing, a whiff of pessimism and a chunk of optimism - all at the same time.

He remembered what the old man had said: "You're focusing on what's not working." He decided to focus on the feelings of relief, doing the right thing and optimism.

His thinking cleared up and a large weight lifted from him. Just then, his brain started to chime in: Fears of jail, losing everything...losing Melinda, his mom. Everything.

Breathe. Breathe.

He decided to go for a run. He knew that would be something to settle him down.

Midway during his run, his thoughts cleared. He remembered the conversation with the old man from earlier.

"Find your thing, Brian. Find your thing."

Tears welled up from within him. Then, he started to smile. He had found his thing, running. He actually always had his 'thing,' he had just gotten so busy with "doing" things that he had forgotten.

"Your brain can be your ally or your enemy. You choose, Brian."

A broad smile crossed his face, along with the sudden urge to call Melinda.

"Hello," she said.

"Hi, it's Brian."

"I know," she said.

"Would you be up for dinner tonight?" My treat.

Pause.

Breathe.

"I'm not sure, Brian. Why?"

"No reason really, I just want to see you," he said.

"Okay... O'Malley's?"

"Sure. Seven?"

"Okay, Brian. See you then."

He took a deep breath and headed for the motel.

Who was that old man, he wondered and *What was that song? It was so familiar...*

He filed his thoughts away as he pulled into the parking lot. He showered and got dressed. He had several hours before dinner so he decided to head downtown and people watch.

He had forgotten what it was like to just hang out, to not "Do" anything. Suddenly, a wave of guilt came over him and his phone rang. It was his mom. He let it go to voicemail. Next, Chuck called, several friends from Redmond, a "Private Number" and another he had never heard of. He let them all go to voicemail.

He mused, *The old man's right! It's almost as if when I'm on the right track, things start to test me, to see if I mean business.*

They met at O'Malley's, after all, it was their favorite place. Melinda was dressed in a white satin blouse, nice slacks and her hair pulled back to reveal her radiant features.

She's so beautiful, he thought.

"Hi."

"Hi."

Brian pecked her on the cheek.

"So, how are things?" he said jokingly. They both laughed.

"I'm good Brian, I'm good. How are you?"

"Better." He hesitated to tell her about all his experiences, especially the one with his father and the old man.

He let out a sigh, "Jerry passed away last Wednesday."

"Oh my, gosh, Brian. I'm sorry. How are you?" For the first time in years he actually heard her. She really meant it and wanted to know how he was doing. He realized that for so many years he didn't even hear her, really. He had forgotten what a good friend and ally she was. His heart grew warm and he began to sweat a bit.

"I'm okay. There's been quite a bit going on actually. I'm working it through. It doesn't seem right to download everything right now, until we sort us through, you know."

"I understand. I do love you Brian. That's never changed."

"More warmth in his heart. He remembered the old man's advice about asking direct questions, even and "especially" if you're afraid of the answer. It was an opportunity for him to learn, to grow.

"What happed Melinda? To make you want to spend time with Chuck."

Brian braced himself for what was next, then his heart grew warm, as if it was taking over. He was present, listened and cared. It was as if he realized this wasn't about him... even though it was.

"Ever since you started that Mobile Tech business you became distant. You were consumed by it. You weren't present to me like you were before. We talked, but stopped talking, you know what I mean?"

Brian took a deep breath. "Tell me more," he asked.

"It's as if you tuned and tapped me out. It was like I was in your life, but no longer relevant. You started spending so much time at work, sixty, seventy, even eighty hours a week, and then you started drinking... quite a bit."

She's right, he thought. *I was so consumed by getting somewhere I wasn't around for where I was. I was entrenched in the future, wanting to retire, and not living my life. I wasn't even being me.*

I missed out on so much.

Suddenly, it occurred to him that Melinda was on his side - she wasn't an adversary. No matter what happened between them, what she was saying was for him, for him to grow. He realized and appreciated what a great listener Melinda was. She was looking at him, waiting patiently. So present. She was so present.

He sighed, "Thank you. Would you tell me more?"

"Sure. It's like you lost yourself, Brian, and I lost you, too. I think you were so caught up in being something you weren't, you messed up your internal GPS. You chased the money and forgot you."

Brian realized he was full. Meaning, he had more than enough to sit with and digest for right now. Anymore wouldn't sink in.

"Thanks Melinda, for saying that. I appreciate your honesty. I'll sit with it and I think you're spot on."

As he looked into her eyes, he noticed she was tearing up.

"I'm sorry," she said. "I truly am."

She pulled a small tissue out of her purse and gently wiped her nose.

"I'm sorry I started seeing Chuck, Brian. He was there and listened and helped fill that need. In looking back, I wish I had talked to you first about things, directly. I mentioned it here and there, but I never sat down with you and told you what I thought, how I felt and how important it was. I'm sorry.

"I want you to know that I told Chuck I'm no longer talking to him. If I see him I'll be civil, but I'm no longer sharing things with him. That door is closed – by me – no matter what happens between us. It was wrong for him to approach me and wrong for me to let him in, for me to give him my heart."

Brian's heart began to ache again and tears formed, for him now.

"Okay, Melinda. Okay."

"I'm not hungry, are you?"

"Not really."

"What do you say we table this and go for a walk, just you and me? No talking about mistakes or what happened for the rest of the night, okay?"

"Okay, Brian. Yes."

Brian left a twenty on the table as a tip for the table time and explained to the waiter they had changed their minds.

"No problem," the waiter said.

As they walked along together, they found their way to a nearby pond. Melinda gently put her arm around his and drew him close. Everything felt so right to him.

He realized that when he was present, other things didn't leak in. It created a barrier to worry, to fear. It occurred to him that when he thinks about the myriad of problems he had, even if he was trying to solve them, doors would open to more worry, to more negative thinking.

He even noticed that he needed to be careful how he went about thinking of this insight. "Negative thinking," in most any form, can open the flood gates and make his life very, very difficult

What was important right now was the "right now," and currently he was with his wife, Melinda. That is exactly where he would put his focus.

They walked around for several hours, reminiscing and sharing things from the past. Then, it was as if a door opened. She started sharing her dreams and fears, how she was afraid to fail at work and that her dad would stop loving her. She mentioned how sometimes she even doubted she was good enough for Brian. She said how much she appreciated how nice, gentle, caring and strong he was.

The conversation continued and as they walked. He felt like he knew her, and himself, in a different way. He shared how he was experiencing his mother as self-absorbed and how he let go of his dream to be a doctor when he was a kid, to please her. He told her how intimidated he was of Melinda's dad and how he thought he wasn't good enough for her... that he didn't have the money her dad did.

It was a magical walk. Both shared from the depths of their soul and neither one tried to fix the other. They listened, walked and supported each other in a loving way that they had never done before. Brian felt as though his heart was bigger than a week ago... he felt it and it was full.

They ended their get together around 12:30 that night with a long, tender hug. Their breathing coincided, blended and their bodies fit wonderfully together.

"Good night, Beautiful," he whispered to her as he kissed her on the lips.

"Good night, Brian," she said.

They got into their cars and went their separate ways.

That night, the dream for Brian showed up again. The second one. This time, though, he was still in Maui, but when he returned home that night, he was met by his beauty, Melinda. All was right in the world.

12

He woke up refreshed and rejuvenated. He went for a quick run, showered and went to check his emails. Mr. Ang had requested he call him at his earliest convenience.

Brian checked in with himself and felt a bit of panic.

Breathe, Brian. Breathe.

Okay, I need to grab some food and clear my mind before this call. Humm, that even feels right.

He went to his favorite diner, looking forward to a Denver omelet and some O.J. He might even see the old man again, it's been a while.

Sure enough, there he was, sitting at his usual booth. The old man was talking to a youngster this time. Brian's breath got stuck in his throat. It was his son, from the dream on the cruise.

He sat in the booth in front of them, making eye contact with the old man. "Listen, Brian," the old man said. "Nothing your dad said is about you. I know it sounds weird right now. It's not your fault. He's mean and it's not your fault he drinks so much."

Brian Jr. piped in, "I thought everybody's dad drank like him. When we go out to dinner or things, I see other dads drinking. They get really drunk, too."

"That may be true, son, but it may not be the best choice. You see, when we drink and get drunk a part of us leaves our body. It's like we go on autopilot. Do you know what that is?"

"Sure, I've seen it on cartoons and stuff. It's like a computer that drives."

"Exactly. The thing is, when we get drunk, our brain and our feelings just don't work right. You see?"

"Yes, I guess. But, I figured if I was just a better kid, he'd stop. He's got a lot on his mind. He works so much. I don't want to be a burden."

"Brian, you're not a burden. It's normal for children to do things that take up their parent's time. That's part of being a mom or dad. Unfortunately, sometimes the mom and dad try to make their kids feel guilty in order to change them. Then, the kids change to make their parents happy. The children lose who they are that way, see?"

"Kinda," he paused. "Well, no, not really."

"Okay, let me put it another way. What's your favorite color?"

"Easy peasy. Yellow."

"Great! Have there been times when you wanted something yellow and you were told, 'You really don't want that.'"

"Yes, quite a bit actually. Mommy does that more than Dad."

"Okay. Then, what happens in your brain?"

"I hear my brain voice say, 'Be a good boy. Don't make her angry,' and I stop wanting the yellow one."

"Is it true you stop wanting it or is it more like you force yourself to take the other?"

"Force myself."

"See? That's where it starts. We start to lose ourselves over simple things. Then it grows and grows and grows."

Big Brian took the napkin from beneath his silverware and wiped the tears from his face. They were flowing and flowing. His heart was breaking open again.

"That's enough for now," the old man said. "Go play, okay?"

"Okay. Thanks Grandpa!" he said, and he shot out of the booth and trotted out the door. "Woohoo!!!"

It took Brian a few minutes to collect himself. He was trembling. Memories started flooding in. Memories of all the things he had changed to make his mom and dad happy. Memories of anger, too, which he didn't connect to his changing for them until right now. He never wanted to go into the tech industry. He was doing it because of what Jerry had said about computers and his mom saying, "You'll be a fine entrepreneur someday. A fine one Brian."

Man, what a week he thought, and then he started laughing.

He scooted into the booth in front of him, but the old man was gone.

Interesting, Brian thought. *Interesting.*

He wished he could just pick up the phone and talk to him.

"Hi, this is Brian. What do I do!?" He started laughing again.

Well, he thought. *Let's start off with breakfast and a few more napkins to help with the crying.*

As he finished his omelet, and the tears subsided, he noticed the fullness of his heart again. He felt like he had run a 10k.

I guess emotions can do that, he thought.

He knew he was ready to call Mr. Ang. He went to his room and called him.

"Hello Mr. Ang, it's Brian Richardson."

"Hi, Brian."

"I wanted to thank you for your honesty, albeit a bit later than I would have hoped."

Breathe. Something good will come out of this. Something good will come out of this.

"My accountant and forensic team took some time and looked over your records again. We agree that the only indiscretion was what you mentioned. We also took into account your new client," he paused. "With that in mind, we wish to move forward with the merger, with two conditions."

"Thank you, Mr. Ang. What would those be?"

"The first is that Chuck resigns his position. He still has not come forward as you have and we are aware that he knew of the indiscretion. The second is that you remain on board as an aide to me, the CEO of the merged companies."

"If I may Mr. Ang, why are you asking that I stay on board?"

"While your deception was ill advised, it takes a strong man to admit his mistakes, especially with the threat of prison on his doorstep. You have character, Mr. Richardson, that's why."

Brian paused for a few seconds. He checked in with himself. While the thought of being his aide sounded great, something was still off inside. It didn't quite feel right and he couldn't put his finger on it.

"Thank you Mr. Ang. May I ask your permission to take 48 hours to sit with this?"

"Absolutely, Brian. I look forward to hearing from you."

"Thank you Mr. Ang," and he hung up.

Brian's head started to spin. He started to list the pros and cons, the fact that it was "a great opportunity," he could buy the home he wanted, treat Melinda so much better, buy her things and they could get a place in Maui and retire.

Wait a minute!

He realized his thoughts were hollow. He was in a flat spin, no traction on anything, there was no real feeling to any of it. None. . Sure, there was excitement with the thoughts of those things, but it was like a cookie that was hollow inside.

He really just searching for a reason to justify what he already knew.

He took a breath again.

Patience, he thought. *Patience. I have 48 hours.*

It occurred to him - it struck him really. The dream with him at the cruise paralleled the dream with him on the boat that sank. He was the little boy that the old man had talked to. It was him, and if he didn't change, he would have another boy just like him - he would repeat the pattern. His boy would grow up like him and have a child, and so on and so on. Unless he changed – permanently - the cycle would continue. If he didn't, he would create more little boys like him. Boys that changed for their parents, that didn't pursue their dreams and became people they didn't want to be.

Breathe, Brian. Breathe.

He woke up the next morning, his brain clear and his body refreshed. He went for his run, which was now becoming part of his routine, as was his morning breakfast.

He woke up knowing that the job with Mr. Ang was not for him. He couldn't quite put his finger on why, he just knew it didn't feel right.

As a matter of fact, he didn't know what he wanted to do. With his life.

13

Chuck called. He picked it up.

"Say, good news. They're going ahead with the merger."

"I heard Chuck, I heard. I'm no longer with the company though. I'll finish up the necessary paperwork. I've resigned."

"Okay, buddy. Ok."

"Chuck, I'm no longer your buddy. When I finish with this part, I never want to see you again." He hung up.

Apparently, Chuck hadn't heard he wasn't with the company either.

Brian had time on his hands. He thought about calling Melinda to spend some time with her, it didn't feel right though. He found himself downtown perusing a second hand book store.

Interesting, he thought. I never go to these places.

He ended up in the self-help section and a book caught his eye.

Who would have thunk, he thought.

He opened the book to the chapter titled, "If you could do anything you wanted and knew you would not fail, what would it be?"

"Easy," he thought.

When he was six he wanted to be a doctor. He was around sick children quite a bit and wanted to help them. He wanted to find a cure for children's illnesses. It was his dream.

Suddenly, he was whisked back in time, to a place in his bedroom where he was playing doctor. "I can fix you," he said to Mr. Whiskers, his teddy bear. His mom walked in. "Brian, what are you doing?"

"I'm a Doctor Mommy. I'm helping kids."

"No. No you're not," she said with a sharp voice. "Doctors get sued, they suffer from malpractice suits and work all their lives. Do you remember what Jerry said, 'Work hard and a man can achieve anything?'"

"Yes."

"Well, you can retire one day. He says that computers are the thing, not doctoring. Besides. You don't really want to help children, do you? You don't want to be a doctor."

"No mommy. No, I guess not."

The tears welled up in Brian's eyes. He dried them off with his sleeve and looked for the bathroom. Once he got the key, he sat down on the toilet and cried. He pulled what seemed like years and years of toilet paper, releasing all his pent up frustration, his hurt feelings and his feelings of not being enough. His heart hurt again.

Will this ever end, he thought. *Ever?*

The tears subsided as did the ache in his heart. He wiped his nose one last time and headed back to the book. He bought it and went back to his rig.

A doctor? I'm too old to go back to school.

Fear welled up inside him. He literally felt his chest tighten.

Damnit. That's not good. Now what?

"Listen Brian. Listen," he heard.

Breathe. Breathe.

He went to the hotel room and started reading the book. The first two chapters were about fear, what it does and how to overcome it. It asked, "What are three things that you are afraid will happen?"

Easy, thought Brian.

Not knowing who I am

Ending up living by the river somewhere with no money

Being alone for the rest of my life

The book suggested he journal about the three questions, and he did. It said to go stream of conscious, to not judge and let the thoughts and feelings grow and flow. It also said to look for "Negative beliefs about yourself, ones that drive the fears." The idea was to uncover what those beliefs are, to "dig" if you will.

After several hours of journaling, and a half a box of Kleenex, here's what he learned:

> He had the habit of giving up on himself, of changing for others.

> He saw how he stopped knowing who he really was when he gave up on his dreams, and each time he let fear win.

> He also got how he reinforced things each time he put himself down or told himself, "I can't."

The fear of living under the bridge somewhere came from a nightmare he had as a kid. It was about being homeless, with no place to live. He sat with that a bit and realized that the dream was really a metaphor, it was about feeling unloved by his parents. Even though he had a roof over his head, he never felt like he had a "home." It was another version of losing himself.

The last one, "Being along for the rest of his life," was another way of looking at leaving himself. You see, the only way he would be alone is if he abandoned himself. By abandoning his thoughts, wants, needs, feelings and dreams, he was actually living alone. That's the only way it would happen.

Imagine a scarecrow in the middle of a corn field. No animation, just there stiff and straight. That was him - if he left himself. No animation, just a body.

Whew, he thought. *I get it. Wait, almost.*

There seemed to be one more piece. His phone rang. It was Mr. Roberts, Melinda's dad. A knot grew in his stomach again, yup. The same knot.

He swiped right. "Hi, Mr. Roberts."

"Hi Brian, do you have a minute?"

"Yes sir."

"Brian, call me Ed, ok?"

"Okay, Ed."

"Listen, I know you love my daughter, that's been clear to me ever since I met you. I wanted you to know that I think you're a good man, I just don't know if you're up to her. Do you know what I mean?"

"No, Sir."

"Well, I've always been able to provide for her and she's become accustomed to that. I don't think you'll be able to do that, even with this merger, you just don't seem to have it in you.   Do you see what I mean?"

Brian took a deep breath. "Sir, may I be candid with you?"

"Ed, call me Ed. Yes, Son, go ahead."

"I'm a good man, and I love your daughter. While I respect your opinion, I don't agree." Brian couldn't believe what was coming out of his mouth. "Yes, you have billions and I don't. I, however, have the love of your daughter, and I in turn love her. I believe that's stronger than any dollar. Besides, the money will come, Ed and it isn't everything. You may lose everything tomorrow... who knows?"

Silence. Long silence. Fifteen seconds that seemed like five minutes.

"Brian, you're wrong. Flat out wrong, you're not good enough for my Melinda," and he hung up.

Brian had just stood up for himself.

What was this new me? I did it with Mr. Ang and now Mr. Roberts.

It felt uncomfortable really, not necessarily wrong, just uncomfortable. Inside, everything felt right. He felt right as rain actually. He was learning to be true to himself, no matter the consequences.

Nice.

14

The next day, things seemed to slow down for Brian. He was enjoying his new routine of a morning run and a nice breakfast. He even added a slow walk several times a day... it helped him calm down and regroup.

He thought about things of late. His stepdad's death, his multi-millionaire status, his wife having an emotional affair with his ex-best friend, and the possibility of ending up in jail. All these things had been a trigger point for him – plus the dreams. He started to connect the dots. As he was sitting there, looking over the view in Logan, he realized that his dreams changed as he changed. He now felt so much more like himself, more aware of who he was and what he wanted.

There was one dream that wasn't changing though, the dream on the cruise ship. It still played the same way, with the exception of the little boy. He no longer took on the beliefs that he was a bad kid or responsible for his father's crankiness and drinking. Melinda still had an affair and he was still bitter. There seemed to be a piece missing.

Growing older and wiser, by what seemed like years in the last few days, he realized his life would tell him what's up. All he needed to do was listen.

That afternoon, he hopped into his rig to meet Melinda. Two minutes into his drive, a semi almost forced him into a guardrail. Once he was through that, he found himself in a five mile backup due to road construction. He pulled into a nearby park and got out. He walked around, focusing on his breathing and "not thinking."

As he settled down, a couple of questions formed in his mind:

Is Melinda right for me? Am I right for her?

The knot formed in his stomach followed by thoughts of the "unknown" if he left her. True, she owned up to her part in the emotional affair she had with Chuck, yet something felt off to him.

"Trust your gut," he heard his real dad say. "Sorry I wasn't there for you," chimed his stepdad and "Listen," from the old man.

Jesus, he thought. *I'm terrified to leave her, yet I don't want to stay because I'm afraid. That's no life to live.*

In that moment he felt like he was at a turning point in his life. He saw a vision in front of him, one that clearly showed he didn't have to live his life to please others. He was no longer his mother's son. He was no longer the boy abandoned by his father.

He remembered one of his conversations with the old man, "We all know what we really want deep down. The trick is to get out of our own way. Sometimes, fear of the unknown, fear our brain creates, keeps us stuck."

He met with Melinda later that night. They had a wonderfully long walk and while there was a connection, there was something missing for him - he could feel it. There was a depth that wasn't present, a depth and a trust that he wanted. Now, the question was: Would time create that with her or was it to be with someone else?

He told her what was going on for him. "I understand," she said. "Part of this is that you don't trust me, and I don't blame you. I'm sorry that I took it as far as I did. I also know that I can't make things shift back for you - you'll have to do that. If there's a wall there that doesn't leave, well, that's part of my consequence for choosing to see Chuck. I'm not willing to live like that, though, forever. I'm willing to give it some time, yet if it doesn't shift, I understand."

Brian's heart opened up. He still didn't know if she was the one. Neither did she.

He gave her a peck on the cheek, a long hug and headed back to the motel. On the way home he felt the strong urge to go into the local drug store, you know, the mom and pop one with the eclectic setup.

He found himself in the back of the store and on the shelf, away from the other knick-knacks, were several different sets of hats. There were cowboy hats, baseball hats, fishing hats...and fedoras. There, looking at him was the very same white, blue, beige and yellow blended fedora that the old man had been wearing.

Interesting, he thought. Interesting.

He left the store with the hat in his hand - it didn't seem right to put it on yet. He also knew that deep down, everything would be okay.

He had learned to listen and that his life wanted him to succeed.

Paul has over thirty years of experience in helping people better themselves. For twelve years, he served as a police officer and detective with the King County Sheriff's Department in Seattle, WA. In 1998, he drew upon his experience, rechanneled his efforts and created Peace Enforcement LLC. He has been working to positively impact the lives of adults, children, companies and people of all ages ever since.

Paul provides keynotes, breakouts, workshops, trainings and individual mentoring. Below is a partial list of the many ways he may be of service:

For Companies and Organizations:
Workplace Improvement
Staff Development
Management Skills
Leadership Training
Mentoring

For Parents:
Parent Workshops
Parent Retreats
Presentations on numerous topics, including:

The Value of Positive Structure
Avoiding the Four Negative Parenting Styles
Is it You, or Is it Me?

For Children and Young Adults:
The Peace Enforcement Self Esteem Program
Bullying Prevention
Where Did my Dreams Go?
Positive Choices for a Happier Life
The Language of Leadership

For those that Work with Children:
The Peace Enforcement Self Esteem Provider Program

For more information or to arrange to have Paul speak at your location or conference, contact us at:

Peace Enforcement LLC
(877) ITS PAUL
877- 487-7285
www.PaulFigueroa.com

56889830R00054

Made in the USA
Lexington, KY
01 November 2016